Roland Harvey's DRAWING BOOK

SCHOLASTIC INC.

New York   Toronto   London   Auckland   Sydney
Mexico City   New Delhi   Hong Kong

ISBN 0-439-10846-2

Text and illustrations copyright © 1996 by Roland Harvey.
All rights reserved. Published by Scholastic Inc.,
555 Broadway, New York, NY 10012, by arrangement with
Scholastic Australia Pty Limited. SCHOLASTIC and associated logos are trademarks and/or registered trademarks of Scholastic Inc.

12 11 10 9 8 7 6 5 4 3 2 1   9/9 0 1 2 3 4/0

Printed in the U.S.A.   08

First Scholastic printing, November 1999

Typeset in 15pt Helvetica.

Contents

I f I were asked to describe something, I would probably draw it. If I had to remember something, I would probably draw it. One of my favourite ways of relaxing is to sit quietly and draw or paint—even my concentration in meetings and lectures is much better if I doodle! Would you be surprised then, to hear that I love my job as an illustrator?

One of the best things about illustrating is the range of opportunities that it offers. There are so many products that involve illustrating—books, greeting cards, posters, advertising, animation, television and multimedia are just a few examples. It can be serious, funny or both. And then there is the equipment—pen, pencil, paint, chalk, rag, wood, watercolour—the list goes on and on.

On top of all this there seems to be no limit to the number of styles from which we can choose, to suit our particular talents and personalities.

Better still, we can invent or develop one for ourselves.

And if that's not enough, there are 7951 850 766 different things to draw, paint or describe (at the time of writing).

So after all that, I should introduce you to this book! It's about one person's approach (mine) to the challenge of illustrating; and it talks about a lot of the things which I have found useful while illustrating.

I have tried not to make too many rules, but have talked about some of the things which really do help if you understand them. If some sections do interest or excite you, there's plenty more that you can learn by reading specific books on those subjects.

That's one step on the road to working out your own style. And that's what will make you a person in demand! Your style is the key to a really exciting hobby, or even a career.

Styles

How many illustrating styles are there?

Even I have three or four. Take a look in a library or a bookshop and you will soon see how many ways there are to describe a scene by drawing. Not right or wrong ways—just different ways. And this is a very important point:

Formal, old-fashioned style

if you keep drawing, and looking, and trying, you will find a style and a kind of work which suits you and your particular talents and interests!

↑ see 'perspective'; eggs

funny style

serious technical style

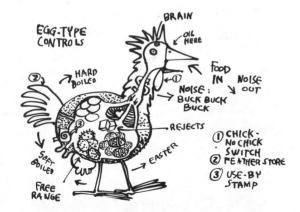

EGG-TYPE CONTROLS

BRAIN

OIL HERE

FOOD IN

NOISE OUT

HARD BOILED

NOISE: BUCK BUCK BUCK

REJECTS

SOFT BOILED

EASTER

① CHICK - NO CHICK SWITCH
② FEATHER STORE
③ USE-BY STAMP

FREE RANGE

TECHNICAL DIAGRAM OF A CHOOK

A DEAD SERIOUS STYLE

DRAWN BY: DATE:

A happy free range chook

soft, pretty style

'Stylised'

CAREERS

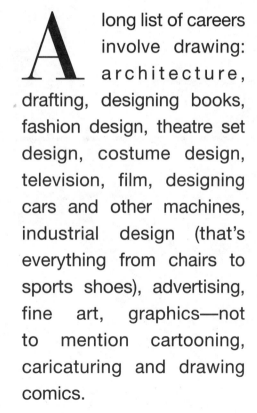

A long list of careers involve drawing: architecture, drafting, designing books, fashion design, theatre set design, costume design, television, film, designing cars and other machines, industrial design (that's everything from chairs to sports shoes), advertising, fine art, graphics—not to mention cartooning, caricaturing and drawing comics.

I DON'T MEAN TO BE NEGATIVE BUT YOU'RE ONLY TWO FEET OFF THE GROUND

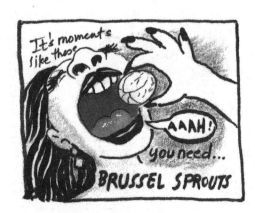

It's moments like these

AAAH!

you need...

BRUSSEL SPROUTS

There are all sorts of pens and nibs.

They don't smudge (once the ink is dry!) and if you use waterproof ink you can paint over the drawing with washes of ink or watercolour. These are the ones that I find most useful:

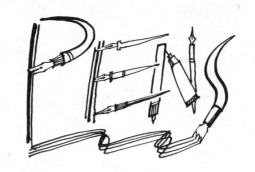

HEY!

WATCH IT...

HEY! STAY ON THE PAGE!

DRAWING WITH PEN AND INK

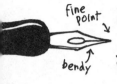

fine point

bendy

Dip nibs make great drawing pens. Softer, bendier nibs give more character than stiffer ones. They're also good for lettering like this.

Thicker nibs are good for larger drawings.

Square stubs are good for this but not for drawing. ———— —— —— ——

Calligraphy nibs are good for decoration but not for drawing...

Can be different thicknesses

Double nibs can do amazing things but not drawing!!

DOCTOR - I'M ALMOST BESIDE MYSELF

YOU NEED GLASSES

Looks like he drew that with a COMB!

music pens are fun for drawing

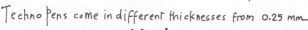

Techno pens come in different thicknesses from 0.25 mm ——

0.35 **0.5 0.7 and thicker and thicker.** They draw well but without character.

BRUSH PENS are great for expressive lines

NASA has developed a pen that writes in zero gravity!

NOT MUCH USE IF YOU CAN'T REACH IT!

Inks are either waterproof or soluble. If you like, you can use soluble ink which creates interesting effects when you leave it to dry and then wet it.

Like this:

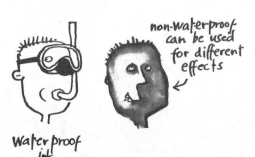

Waterproof ink

non-waterproof can be used for different effects

Felt pens are very cheap and convenient. You can choose water-based or spirit-based pens.

Spirit-based pens are more lasting and can be painted over.

Most felt pens are good for quick sketching.

chisel point markers — good for writing or REALLY BIG calligraphy, but not for drawing.

hard tip felt pens are fine for drawing — don't spatter — but not as crisp as ink.

ballpoints are good for doodling!

The ORIGINAL!

Pens are named from the latin word 'PENNA', which means 'feather', because that's what the first pens were!

Exercise N° 2

Make your own quill pen.

1. Get a feather! (one that's big enough to hold like a pen)

2. Cut the tip off like this with a penknife.

3. Slit the tip. →

4. Dip and draw!

TIP: OSTRICH feathers can be hard to control

9

MATERIALS
Pencils

PENCILS are made of clay and graphite or carbon.

The more graphite, the darker the line, the _softer_ the lead. Soft pencils like 6B, 4B, 2B are good for drawing like this...

Light, or **hard** pencils (6H, 4H, 2H) are good for fine light lines. It helps to have the right lead for your job.

HELP

200

150 75

WATERPROOF SHARKPROOF 50 x 25 TIMBER

WHITE PAINTED WATERPROOF BOARD 9 MM THICK.

MICRO PENCILS ARE GREAT FOR FINE DRAWING LIKE THIS!

CHISEL

FLAT

'CLUTCH' PENCILS TAKE 2 mm LEADS OF ALL KINDS

You can get different effects by sharpening your lead in different ways

FINE POINT

Lead pencil drawings smudge really easily—especially soft leads.

I often smudge mine with my arm or hand.

You can avoid smudging by:
- working down from the top of the page
- covering drawings with smooth paper as you go
- spraying drawings with fixative
- keeping fingers off the page.

Oilstick (solid oil paint), pastel, charcoal, crayon, conté are all for big bold drawings. You will get different effects depending on the paper you use.

MORE MATERIALS

Drawn with Umbrella + Chewy

oil stick ... good for large drawing and painting. Takes time to dry.

charcoal or burnt stick ... you can even make your own!

Pastel ... lovely soft colours, smudging can add texture.

crayon and oil Pastel ... half-way between crayon and pastel.

Conté ... sort of chalky charcoal!

umbrella and chewing gum ... not good for anything much except annoying art teachers. CAUTION: Can affect flavour.

Exercise Nº 3

Try to shade from dark to light to dark again with an even continuous tone. Try it with a few different pencils and points and papers!

Paper can be made from different things to give it different qualities.

It can be smooth-surfaced or about a million different kinds of rough.

I'm *really* rough!

If you're painting over a drawing, you need watercolour paper, which also comes in smooth and textured varieties. Unless it's very thick, you'll need to tape it down or shrink it to stop it wrinkling.

A good combination is water-colour pencil with plain water washes on watercolour paper.

PAPER for INK

feeling a bit furry today

For pencil drawings, you can choose the kind of paper for the effect you want.

I'm smooth.

I'm drawn on fabric textured paper

I like using smooth, clay-coated paper for ink drawing. The slippery surface makes quick lines easy, and they don't 'bleed' (go furry).

Textured papers give a very different result to smooth drawing papers.

Exercise 4
• Collect as many different paper types as you can.
• Try various things... pen, felt pen, pencil, charcoal etc on each and see the results
• Keep it for future reference.

Shipwreck 1. and shipwreck 2. are painted on smooth (left) and rough (right) papers.
You can see the different textures you get.
Rough is also better for drying socks.

BIRDSEYE

SECTION
(what you don't see)

GROSS

Caricature

my style

elephants don't do this.

COMBI LIGHT, SHOWER AND BROLLY HOLDER

ROTATING GLASSES RACK

SNACK RACK

PAINT DISPENSER

MOUTH-HELD ANTPROOF EASEL AND MUSICAL INSTRUMENT

WATER STORING 'COOLAPANTS'

TECHNICAL 'The Complete Artist'
Roland Harvey's LITTLE PAINTER SET

There are as many drawing styles as there are individuals. I bet you have at least one of your own.

Things that make a difference to illustration style are: realism or the ridiculous, humour, softness, sharpness, boldness, simplicity, detail, roughness (or vigour), precision . . . the list goes on! This book is about one way of illustrating—my particular approach to communicating with you.

I draw in different styles, depending on what the drawing is for. The reason for drawing can be to inform, to show there's a different way of looking at something, or to make your audience laugh. Or it can be because when I paint something like a boat, or the sea, or a lighthouse, I'm escaping— I'm really there!

REALISTIC
...with little jokes hiding.

13

In most of these drawings you will find the same things—humour, detail and a sense of ridiculousness (I made up that word). I call the style I use most 'bird's-eye'. It's good for setting a scene or for creating a lot of detailed action—like Nicholas nicking Nick's knickers in the drawing opposite.

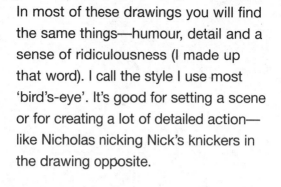

In a section drawing, I can spy on everyone, show what's happening next door, under the ground and in the air.

I also love drawing ridiculous things that can't really work, and gross people or caricatures.

I've tried to work out what has led me to these styles. The little jokes pop up even when I'm doing a serious drawing, so I think it's that my mind is relaxed and allows some other part of my brain to 'come out'. The same thing happens when I'm washing up or driving a long distance, so I note these ideas down too.

The other factor is to do with the way I understand and remember things. If I can't see 'the complete picture', or everything around what I am drawing, I can't understand how it works. So, while I was studying architecture I would draw the building and everything around it—the big picture.

15

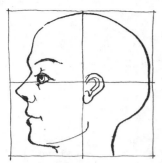

Faces:
Shape and Proportion

So why this bit about proportion?

If we know the basics about what makes a baby's face and body different from a teenager or adult, we can make our baby a baby, even when we've exaggerated it or changed it to suit our style.

AGES. As the body ages, the face changes not only in size but in proportion.

IMPORTANT NOTE... [A] to [E] Real people do NOT look like this.

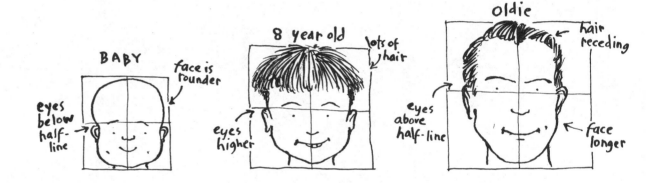

BABY — face is rounder — eyes below half-line

8 year old — lots of hair — eyes higher

oldie — hair receding — eyes above half-line — face longer

EXPRESSIONS

Add hair — and warts — A good example of why I don't draw real people.

content   happy   cheery   sad   disappointed   cold

scared   worried   sneaky   furious   serene   sleepy

But maybe we don't want to draw real people. Perhaps we want to exaggerate the shapes that make up the faces and draw gross or funny people . . .

To do this, you can experiment with basic shapes:

then, with **WHERE** you put things.

After that, you can mix them up again.

Now look at combinations of shapes.

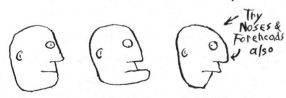

Try Noses & Foreheads also

Just changing a nose, forehead or chin changes personality completely.

A smile can mean different things...

The older you get, the more wrinkles you get.

Look at the faces around you and observe where the lines are, and which ones go with which.

Moving wrinkles about can completely change a character's personality.

If there were only four kinds of forehead wrinkles, four kinds of eye wrinkles, four kinds of mouth and nose wrinkles, four differently shaped heads, four hairstyles, four different chins and noses, you could still draw 16 384 different faces.

The same goes for eyes:

Same face ... different eyes!

* Not recommended without medical advice.

SPOTTER'S SPOT:

See if you can see someone who **LAUGHS UPSIDE-DOWN**.

17

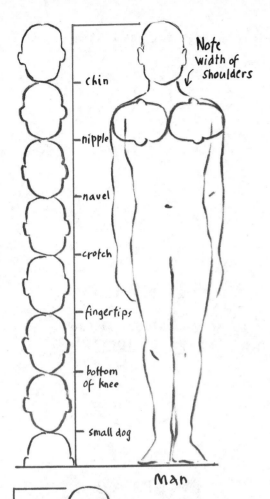

chin
nipple
navel
crotch
fingertips
bottom of knee
small dog

Note width of shoulders

Man

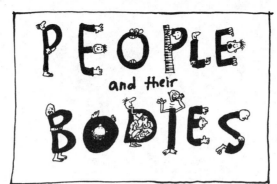

PEOPLE and their BODIES

We're not here to draw real people but, as with the faces, it helps to understand real people's proportions.

It's really useful to look at different people's posture and how people change with age and weight.

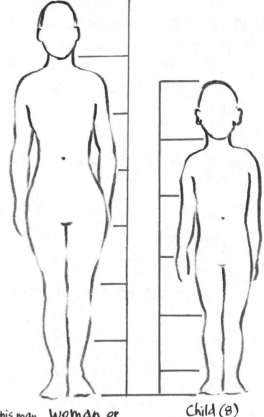

Child (8)

I don't understand muscles

I drew this man on the beach at Byron Bay.

Woman or teenager

A general rule for drawing the human body in proportion is that an average man's height is equivalent to seven and a half times his head height (see above).

A twelve-month-old child is only four times their head height. (Note how the navel is in the centre.) A woman or teenager is about seven times their head height and an eight-year-old child is about five and a quarter times their head height. Remember the height is always measured by the person's own head.

How many of your heads high are you?

Child (12 mths)

Bodies show as much expression as faces. They change with weight, mood, age, personality, build,

balance, action, sex, position & more. On top of that, you can distort and exaggerate them, or

make them up. You can suggest even more about them by the kind of lines you use... bold; timid;

speedy. Exaggerating any of people's characteristics is fun. So experiment! Try to draw bodies

I think it's a first for mankind!

in different positions and movements. Draw quickly, work over it again. Be adventurous!

19

I try to feel what my drawing would feel. Watch what your body does in different moods and situations.

Watch people in trains, on the beach, playing sport . . . everywhere.

people in

People Interacting

Stick Figures

Drawing stick figures can be a big help in getting the action you want.

Movement

Quick sketchy lines can suggest movement. Try to follow the true direction of the movement.

Look out for ways of sitting:

Actions and Reactions

People in groups don't usually behave like this...

what else can they do? They can **Interact**.

Aggro   fear   Concern   Confusion

What are these people saying to each other?

Focusing attention

You can focus attention where you want it by persuading your crowd to look there.

HANDS

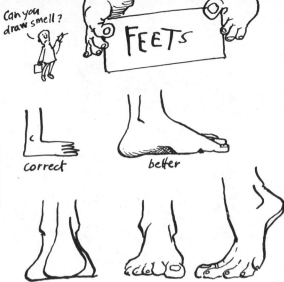

^ wrong.

FACTS:
① It's harder to draw without them.
② You could go your whole life without drawing one (by cheating like me)
③ If you REALLY want to, the best way is to:

- Look at your hand.
- Look at the basic shapes which make it up...
- Practise drawing hands from different angles, doing different things.

I often need to draw hands holding things

or playing instruments.

you can't see her thumb at all

By far the best way is to observe and practise!

people: Hard Bits

Hands, feet, necks, muscles . . . hard to draw but really useful if you want to get expression into your drawings.

66'

Because I generally draw quite small or simple figures, I don't need to worry too much about hands and feet. Even so, they can still be very expressive.

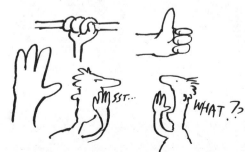

SST...   WHAT..?

FEETS

Can you draw smell?

correct   better

Take a good look at your feet and draw them in as many positions as you can. Then draw your friend's feet from different angles.

NECKS, PLEASE!

curved..   straight   thick

Elegant

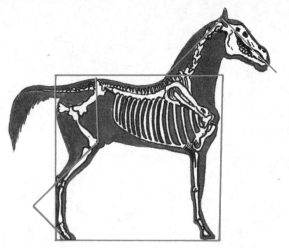

To draw animals' shapes it helps to understand their bone structure. Look at the angles of the neck, head and back legs. This should help get the proportions right.

Now look at different kinds of horses.

Clydesdale

Shetland Pony

Arabian

Thoroughbred

They all have slightly different proportions. Can you work out the differences?

ANIMALS and their characteristics

Animals' bones make them move in particular ways. Or does the way they move make them a particular shape?

Anyway, there seem to be features in each animal that make them recognisable. Have a look at these examples and then study other animals to discover their characteristics.

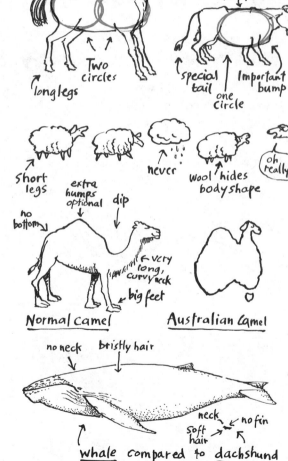

Enough about horses! Other creatures have shapes of their own...

ENOUGH OF HORSES

WE HAVE SHAPES TOO

EQUAL RIGHTS

I AM NOT A HORSE

SNAILS ARE PEOPLE TOO

Round end curvy neck

pointy end

assorted bumps

flat back

Two circles

long legs

special tail

one circle

Important bump

short legs

extra humps optional

never

dip

Wool hides body shape

oh really?

no bottom

a very long, curvy neck

big feet

Normal Camel

Australian Camel

no neck

bristly hair

neck

no fin

soft hair

whale compared to dachshund

Note these important differences.

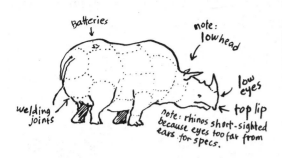

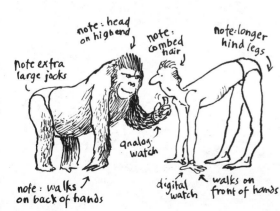

ANIMALS... WHAT'S THE DIFFERENCE?

Animals differ from one another in many ways. Not only because of their bones and shapes but because of their skin, hair, fur, eyes, ears, beaks, tails—even their personalities. It helps to emphasise these features when drawing them.

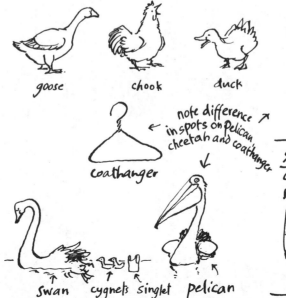

goose   chook   duck

coathanger

swan   cygnets   singlet   pelican

Dogs and Cats...

Afghan Hound

Pointer

Bull Terrier

Note the different proportions of head, leg and muscle of the different cats...

Spot the difference! Even the spots can help make your drawing look more recognisable. These belong to:

jaguar   leopard   cheetah

23

what is he talking about?

dunno?

Complicated ANIMALS!

As with people, balancing your animals is important, or they will fall over.

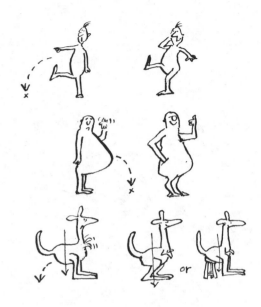

Animals such as kangaroos can be difficult to draw, especially if they are hopping, jumping or doing things they're not supposed to.

To make it easier, work out the basic shapes first. Then you can arrange them as you like.

Once you've worked out how they are put together, you can make them do other things or caricature them as you like.

lend us five bucks?

No way

front   back

This big red needs two circles for his body

Note his big chest + shoulders

Smaller models are a different shape

same

You think I really look like this?

Big Red   Walleroo   Bettong

24

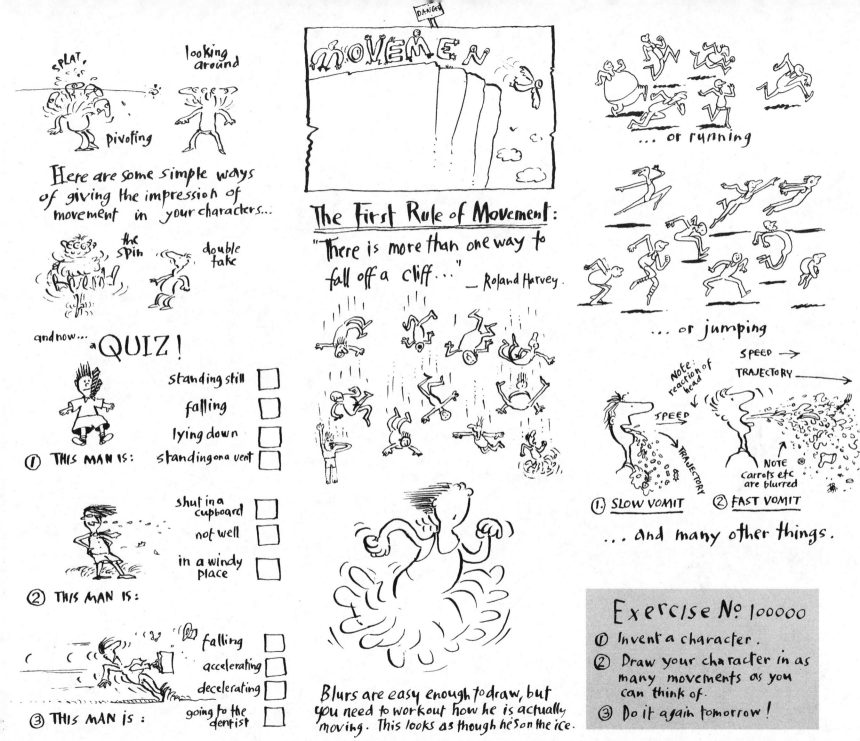

SPLAT

pivoting

looking around

Here are some simple ways of giving the impression of movement in your characters...

the spin

double take

and now... a QUIZ!

① THIS MAN IS:

standing still ☐
falling ☐
lying down ☐
standing on a vent ☐

② THIS MAN IS:

shut in a cupboard ☐
not well ☐
in a windy place ☐

③ THIS MAN IS :

falling ☐
accelerating ☐
decelerating ☐
going to the dentist ☐

DANGER

MOVEMEN

The First Rule of Movement:

"There is more than one way to fall off a cliff..." — Roland Harvey.

Blurs are easy enough to draw, but you need to work out how he is actually moving. This looks as though he's on the ice.

... or running

... or jumping

Note: reaction of head

SPEED →

TRAJECTORY →

SPEED

TRAJECTORY

NOTE carrots etc are blurred

①. SLOW VOMIT   ②. FAST VOMIT

... and many other things.

Exercise № 100000

① Invent a character.
② Draw your character in as many movements as you can think of.
③ Do it again tomorrow!

ANIMAL MOVEMENT

BIRDS

Birds have different ways of flying and different shaped wings for hovering, gliding, soaring etc. Watch how they land. and sing.

tail up when climbing!

tail down when descending!

Never

outer petrel

Low-speed kangaroo hop

Tail down: Legs back!

Tail up: Legs forward!

G'day

Never — or

High-speed bound

Hurry!

I'm flat out!

Come on dad!

Horses, like kangaroos, have different movements at different speeds.

Notice how most animals seem to get longer + lower at higher speed — they stretch further with each bound.

See how this horse often has only one foot on the ground.

A REAL MAN

saves on shoe wear

OUR MAN

Watch this!

Stretch stretch

Stretch

creak

Hello, Doctor?

26

Is it better to draw from real life, or from memory? Or from rules? I think it must be different for every person, since every person is different!

My best drawings are done from memory.
If I get stuck or it's a detail bit or a complex technical thing like a saxophone or a motorbike I either:
① Make it up
② Cheat (see P.62)
③ Try to work it out
④ Go and look at one.

eg.

stuck   observe   redraw

SHAPE AND PROPORTION

I think something in your brain records things and then simplifies

OR

rearranges them in the best way for you to draw them.

Observing is especially useful when drawing real people—in getting exactly the look of the eyelids or the shape of the chin.

I think ears should be more muscly

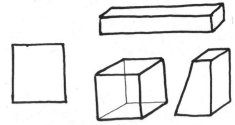

Most things in the known universe

are made up of shapes like these.

It can help in drawing complex

shapes to start with simple ones.

Exercise Nº 27B/1

Pick any 2000 things in your kitchen, and try drawing their basic shape using these circles, cylinders etc.

Probably the main things you remember are the bits that stand out to you, and they're the things to emphasise when you draw it.

One of the most useful things you can do for your drawing is to start observing and remembering what you see.

Driving, walking, shopping, going to the movies — these are really good opportunities to observe shapes and proportions!

One of my very early memories.

No wonder he finds it so hard to wake up in the mornings

Even if we're drawing from memory, it often helps to sort out the basic shapes and proportions first.............. ...... because in drawing we can make ANYTHING happen! So it may not be possible to refer to anything at all.

(See 'perspective', page 40.)

EXERCISE Nº 7691

Take a small sketch pad with you when you go out and quickly sketch the shapes of things you see or details of them. It will be good practice and great for later reference.

 **MORE SHAPES AND PROPORTION**

 **TREES**

some blobs will be behind others

shade see p. 46

Some trees grow into quite regular shapes... others definitely do not.

Trees can grow in layers

note light & shade

Wind can change tree shape

silhouette

The type of strokes or lines you use will tell a lot about the tree too. Experiment with lines,

Some have many trunks...

and bean-shaped blobs... or

very long trunks.

which do have their advantages

CARS & BOATS

1920s Sedan

1930s racer

look for new shapes and proportions.

The shapes of cars and

Some cars had back seats on the outside, called 'Dickie Seats'

Big American car of the 1950s

Little German car you've probably never seen.

There are lots of books on boats. Check the library, or look for magazines with boat pictures in them.

boats have changed <u>heaps</u> over the last hundred years, as technology made new things possible.

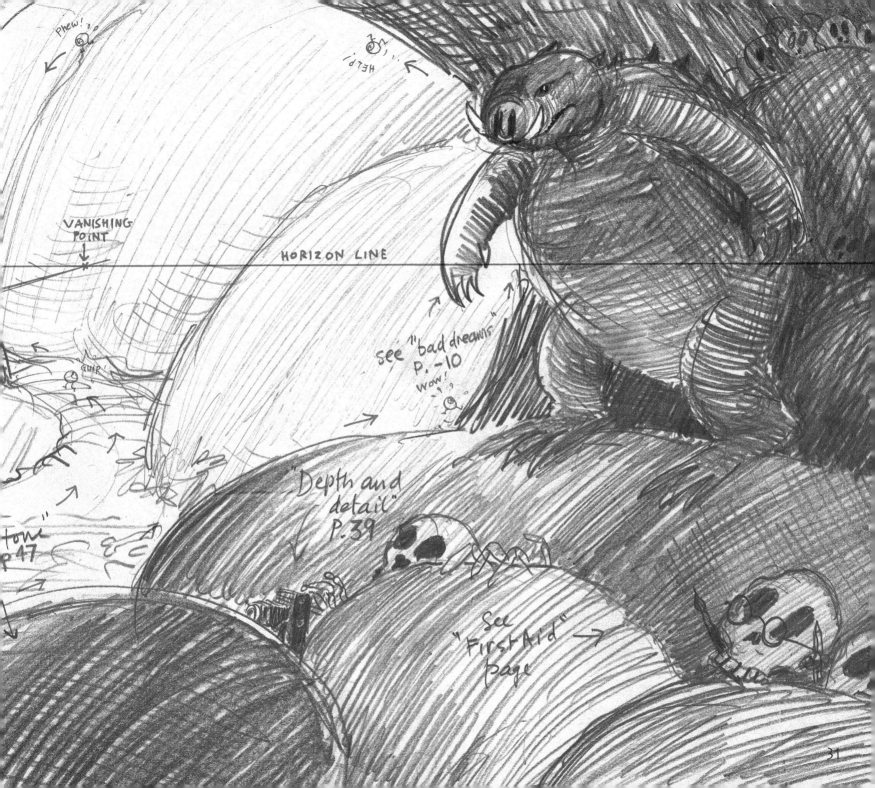

To begin planning we must decide:
"WHAT IS OUR DRAWING TRYING TO DO?"

Are we trying to grab attention and show a simple message?

If so the plan should be to keep the drawing simple, using only the necessary elements to get the message across.

Perhaps we want to puzzle, challenge or entertain.

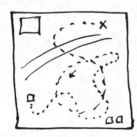

This will need careful thought to be sure that the drawing works as we want.

PLAN NING — why?

Some sort of plan is necessary for every drawing, even if it is only in your head!

A plan helps with things like balance and composition. (These design elements are reflected in the way your eye moves around a picture and comes to rest on certain areas. See pages 36 and 37.)

In book illustration you want all the pages to belong to one another, so planning is helpful.

When drawing tricky shapes like hands, bodies, faces or machines, it helps to rough out proportions and try different approaches. That's planning too.

Are we trying to pass on a lot of information - such as History facts or technical stuff?

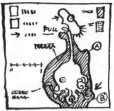

see? Didn't need a plan

If so, do we need to list the items to go in our drawing? Do we need symbols and a legend to show what they mean? How big must it be to show the detail we need?

a result of poor planning →

We may be wanting to create a mood or atmosphere perhaps described in a book.

more bad planning

The atmosphere might be one of peace, excitement, danger, chaos ... Each of these would probably need a different approach.

We can do any number of roughs on scrap paper. sketch the drawing first in pencil and rub it out later. Rule it up carefully and draw over it in free hand.

The most important thing about planning is to work out which method of planning works best for **YOU**.

Often, I can see an illustration in my head, so there's no need for a detailed plan—just a few lines.

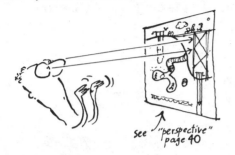

see "perspective" page 40

Another favourite of mine is to draw the key elements first (like a road, a building, a door; that is, the most important bits). Then I start drawing from one of the corners.

I think this works because I use my brain in one way to plan and in another way to do the fun part. So I break down the drawing into two jobs.

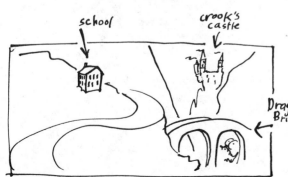

school

crook's castle

Dragon Bridge

PLANNING

Drawing in this way is fun and as I relax, I find little ideas and jokes pop up unexpectedly.

Speaking of relaxing, I think my best drawings are created when I'm testing a new nib, or paper or just doodling— when the drawings have no real purpose.

It seems that you reach into the deepest, most secret parts of the mind when you are just drawing for its own sake. So getting the planning out of the way makes sense doesn't it?

We'll look at composition in a minute (page 36), but we should first work out what it is!

Composition is how a picture is 'composed'—put together, arranged or designed.

If you keep composition in mind when you plan a drawing, you can move the main bits around until the composition works and the picture does what you want it to—leads the viewers to look where you want them to look, to see what you want them to see.

NOTHING

HA HA HA !!

SOMETIMES I GET BLOCKED UP.

I have several secret remedies for this:
1. Go and do something else for a while (preferably something forbidden).
2. Go and play guitar, run, have a tuna malt.
3. Take a whole different approach.
4. Talk to someone (the doctor?) about it.
5. Think: "How would Napoleon draw this?" (or anyone)

33

Developing characters

It is important that characters are recognisable and consistent all the way through the book.

I do lots of roughs, including some ridiculous ones, just to relax—until I hit one I like.

After a little more development, I draw that character from different angles, to 'fix' it in my mind.
I refer to these drawings throughout the book.

34

Planning a book

My favourite way is really part of my style—
I work small.

If I'm working from a manuscript I break it into bite-sized chunks first.

If there's no manuscript or story, I gather all the information together and arrange it in groups. Then I arrange the groups in order, and put them on pages like this . . .

Building shape

Another part of planning a drawing is building shapes. Your first try is not always right, so it's often useful to work the shape over and over to get what you want. Move the head a little, lengthen the chin, should she look over there perhaps?

Exercise No 7½

Try building shapes yourself.
- Start with a basic shape — say a person.
- Lightly & quickly draw heads, arms etc in different actions.
- Draw over your favourite one.

COMPOSITION

There is a simple way to get a feeling of what composition is about. Cut a square in a piece of card and look through it.

You have created a frame which limits your vision. By moving it slowly around, you can compose the picture you see.

You may look up high or down low. It may look better to one side. If it looks unbalanced you can move it to the side.

As the artist, you can create a composition that works best for your drawing.

Composition can happen in many ways. It can be based on shapes like letters . . .

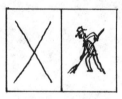

Or, it can be based on simple shapes—circles, ovals, triangles, rectangles.

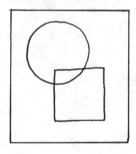

Then again, it may be based on simple curved lines.

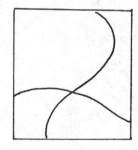

The parts of a drawing can be balanced in a boring way or an exciting way.

(A)

"I SAID: THERE ARE PEANUTS IN MY HARMONICA AGAIN"

(B)

These pictures are both quite balanced but picture B is less boring than picture A.

Another example of this kind of balance is . . .

You will also see that I haven't filled the drawing with lines—there is a lot of white space on the right-hand side. This can be very dramatic and works well with the snow, sky, sand, desert, etc.

Eye paths are a very important part of your picture.

A good eye path leads the viewer into the picture, wanders around a bit and finishes where you want it to—the 'focal point'.

FOCAL POINT

In our picture above the eye does something like this.

Often, when we don't think about eye paths, our drawing ends up with paths anyway. These tend to lead the eye out of the picture, and that's bad.

There are three main things wrong with this picture.

1   The picture is divided in half by the horizon. Higher or lower would be okay.
2   The subject (me) is dead centre (boring) and not on the eye path.
3   Two eye paths lead us past the subject and out of the picture.

WHY AM I STUCK HERE IN THE MIDDLE AND WHAT'S THIS THING STICKING OUT OF MY HEAD?

The worst thing here is that the objects do not interact in any way. Next, the woman is stuck in the centre and too low. The clock is distracting because it is the same size as the woman. The eye paths are leading us out (and so are her eyes).

3D . . . One of the challenges we all have as illustrators is to add a feeling of distance and depth to a picture when we only have a flat page on which to work.

In this drawing, I have shown some tricks to suggest distance and depth.

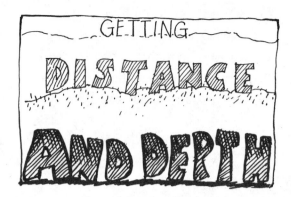

The following secrets are used in this drawing: size, perspective, detail, foreshortening, overlapping, contrast, line and gaps. Spot them (after reading page 39) and win the 'Pictorial depth illusionary technician's execution and theory section' prize.

things to find in this drawing: ① CONTRAST ② PERSPECTIVE ③ SIZE ④ OVERLAPPING ⑤ TONE ⑥ FORESHORTENING ⑦ FOREGROUND DETAIL ⑧ SURFER COW

Size: The most obvious 'trick' is size. The objects drawn larger seem closer to us.

Foreshortening: another way of using size to make this foot seem closer than the body.

CAUTION: DO NOT SCRATCH AND SNIFF.

see 'cheating'. → p62

Detail: On closer objects, show more detail. In real life, too, you see more detail close-up.

WAYS OF GETTING DEPTH IN YOUR PICTURE

There are many tricks we can use to get a feeling of distance and depth in our pictures. Each one makes a big difference—put them together and your drawings will be out of sight.

Contrast: (black against white is an easy example) Strong contrast comes forward. As the subject gets further away, contrast reduces.

Lines touching tend to connect objects

Gaps in lines help separate the objects from each other

Overlapping: even when size suggests closeness, overlapping shows who's closer.

Line: In pictures, the bolder line seems to come forward.

Colour and Tone: Colour can affect distance in our pictures. <u>Warm</u> colours; reds, yellows, browns, seem closer than cool colours like blue, grey, green.

The tone is stronger in the foreground as well... a red car close up will be a brighter tone of red than a red car in the distance! And the shadow further away will be a lighter tone than those close-up.

Perspective: This road probably doesn't really get narrower!

It's a trick called 'perspective' which we use to suggest depth and distance.

See more on page 40, 41 etc. !!

39

To understand perspective, we need to understand 'parallel'. It's like this:

PARALLEL means... 'The same distance apart; never touching or crossing.' OK?

Like: ===========

but not

Like: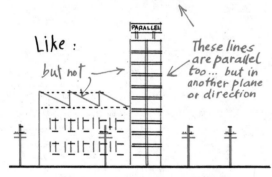

or

Like:

but not

Like:

but not

PARALLEL

These lines are parallel too... but in another plane or direction

Viewer's eye level or horizon or camera level.

DRAWING IN 3-D!

Perspective drawing is the art of suggesting 3-D on a 2-D surface (like this paper.).

THE SIMPLE RULE of PERSPECTIVE

'Things in the same line or parallel seem to recede, converge or disappear to the same point in the distance'. (called the vanishing point or V.P.)

pole-tops do it!

cross bits do it!

Vanishing Point

straight spaghetti does it!

whoops!

trains and smoke do it!

roads do it!

fences and pole bottoms do it!

white lines do it!

signs do it!

GREAT PERSPECTIVE RACE INC. FINISH →

This is SINGLE-POINT PERSPECTIVE

It works when everything is parallel.

① Is the vanishing point always on the HORIZON?

Answer: No! only if the posts and roads are all parallel to one another.

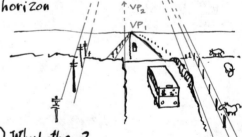

Things NOT PARALLEL have different V.Ps

② What if the road isn't straight?

Answer: There will be different V.P's along the horizon.

See 'Two-point' perspective: P.43

③ What if the road isn't flat?

Answer: Then there will be more than one V.P., not all on the horizon

④ Why bother?

Answer: If you can manage perspective, you can get dramatic and unusual viewpoints right. You can make pictures more interesting and fun. You can make ANYTHING HAPPEN!

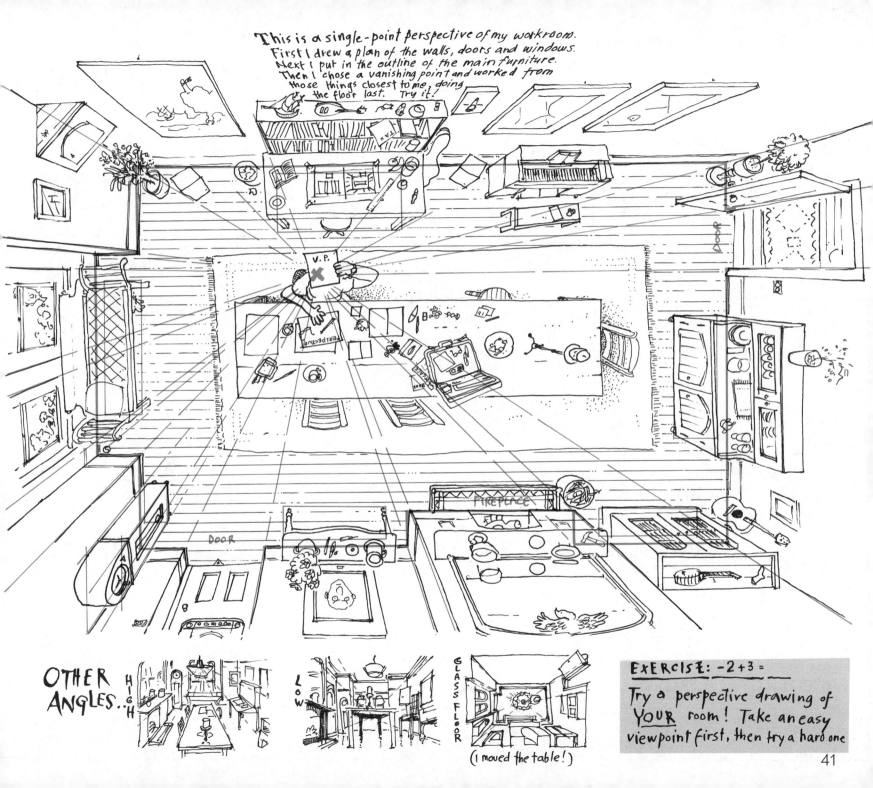

This is a single-point perspective of my workroom.
First I drew a plan of the walls, doors and windows.
Next I put in the outline of the main furniture.
Then I chose a vanishing point and worked from
those things closest to me, doing
the floor last. Try it!

V.P.

DOOR

FIREPLACE

DOOR

OTHER ANGLES.. HIGH

LOW

GLASS FLOOR

(I moved the table!)

EXERCISE: -2+3 =
Try a perspective drawing of
YOUR room! Take an easy
viewpoint first, then try a hard one

Now ... here's another Important Secret.

EYE-LEVEL, CAMERA LEVEL and HORIZON mean the same. True!

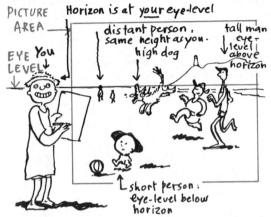

Horizon is at your eye-level

PICTURE AREA

EYE LEVEL

You

distant person, same height as you. high dog

tall man eye-level above horizon

short person: eye-level below horizon

EYE-LEVEL IN PICTURE.

PICTURE AREA

EYE LEVEL

EYE-LEVEL ABOVE PICTURE.

MORE TIPS ON PERSPECTIVE

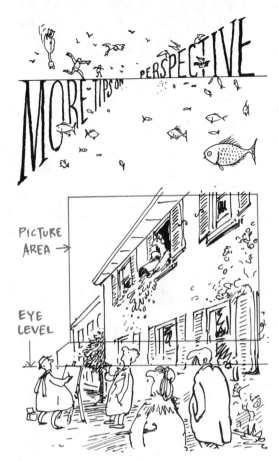

PICTURE AREA

EYE LEVEL

EYE-LEVEL BELOW PICTURE.

You might also notice that fence posts, poles, windows, doors, line up with each other, and their sides are still vertical.

USE SOAP

And now for the **DRAMATIC EFFECTS...**

Giant's View
(high eye-level)

Worm's View
(low eye-level)

For those embarrassing moments when things are not parallel... have different vanishing points.

Some examples...
Two roads going in different directions.

VP1

VP2

MM...MMM... No WIRES.... THIS COULD BE THE NIGHT

You can see how all things parallel — the tops and bottoms of posts, white lines, fences, road edges — all go to the same V.P. on the horizon.

And things parallel to the other road go to their own V.P., on the same horizon (including the wall of the house).

There is no real limit to the number of V.P.s. For example, this fence was put in by a creative farmer:
Note that because all the points are parallel to the flat ground (or plane) the V.P.s are all on the same eye-level line. (horizon)

Notice the horizon is at the viewer's eye-level

VP1   VP2   VP3   VP4   VP5

BEWARE! CREATIVE FARMER

→ VP6
10K

43

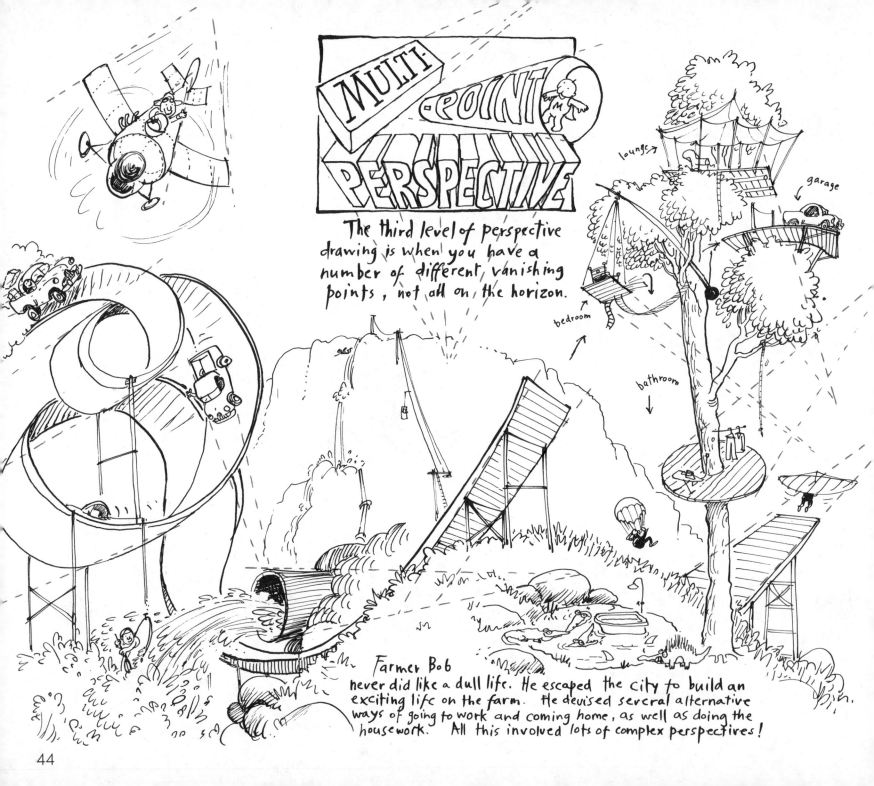

MULTI-POINT PERSPECTIVE

The third level of perspective drawing is when you have a number of different vanishing points, not all on the horizon.

lounge

garage

bedroom

bathroom

Farmer Bob never did like a dull life. He escaped the city to build an exciting life on the farm. He devised several alternative ways of going to work and coming home, as well as doing the housework. All this involved lots of complex perspectives!

Multi-point perspective

Multi-point perspective helps us draw objects in many different planes, creating objects which point in different directions.

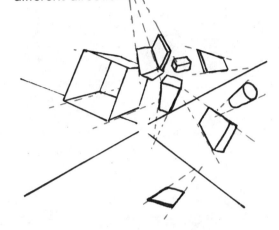

It helps to create a feeling of chaos, disaster, excitement or confusion.

Multi-point perspective is quite easy if you take the objects one at a time—it's really a group of simple perspectives with different viewpoints.

Multi-point perpective can help draw attention to one object . . .

. . . and to add drama.

Cylinders in perspective

Perspective rules also work for cylinders, including wheels.

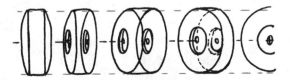

For complicated shapes, always break them up into simple ones, then apply what you've learnt about perspective.

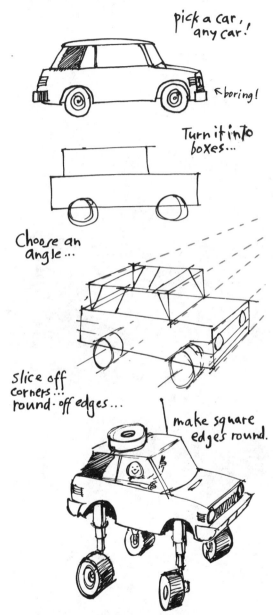

pick a car, any car!

←boring!

Turn it into boxes...

Choose an angle...

Slice off corners... round-off edges...

make square edges round.

We can even get creative!

Line Drawing

Line and solid black

Line and tone (hatching)

To use Tone effectively it helps to understand Light, and where it is coming from (its Source).

The Light source affects the shadows and shading of our subject.

I AM THE SOURCE!

Light source

for example..

How do you do that?

pen or pencil lines

dots

wobbles

hatching and cross-hatching

Each shape has its own areas of light, shade, and shadow...

You can show texture

and reflected light

TONE

To get an illusion of distance into our pictures, there are many things we can do. We already know things get _smaller_ in the DISTANCE. They get less _detailed_. Bull! They seem _greyer_ and _lose colour_ (RED) (watch a car coming towards you — in the distance it will be quite hard to tell what colour it is). These tricks are to do with _Contrast_; that's dark against light, hot against cold, etc. When you look at the drawings below, you will see we can use contrast in Tone as well, to achieve depth and distance.

In these sketches the distance is emphasised by stronger contrast in the foreground and softer in the background.

Silhouettes are effective in setting up a foreground.

Shadows obey the same contrast rule.

Tone can follow the object's shape.

Practise shading lightly too!

Here I am on a cloudy day!

Here's me at Midday...

SHADOW TRICKS

HOW SHADOWS CAN TELL A LOT OF THE STORY

Me flying low...

Flying high...

Here's me at 5.30

Here's me and my naughty dog

On a hill

Against the wall

Me and mum a few years ago...

On tiptoe

jumping

on the run

Arrgh...

backlit

light source to one side

light source in the middle.

at the beach

mum on the rocks

on rough ground

wow

You can see how the light source affects shadows and their shapes.

Unusual points of view make drawings more interesting. I deliberately use a variety of angles, and that makes it more fun for me as well!

One way of making a *map* more interesting (and easier to read) is to turn it into a bird's-eye . . .

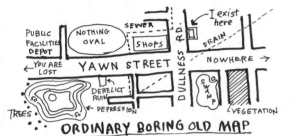

ORDINARY BORING OLD MAP

DELUXE MODEL BIRD'S EYE MAP
These can still be quite accurate.

Another interesting viewpoint. This drawing from 'Milly Fitzwilly's Mousetrap' is really just more perspective drawing (although it was a bit difficult!).

49

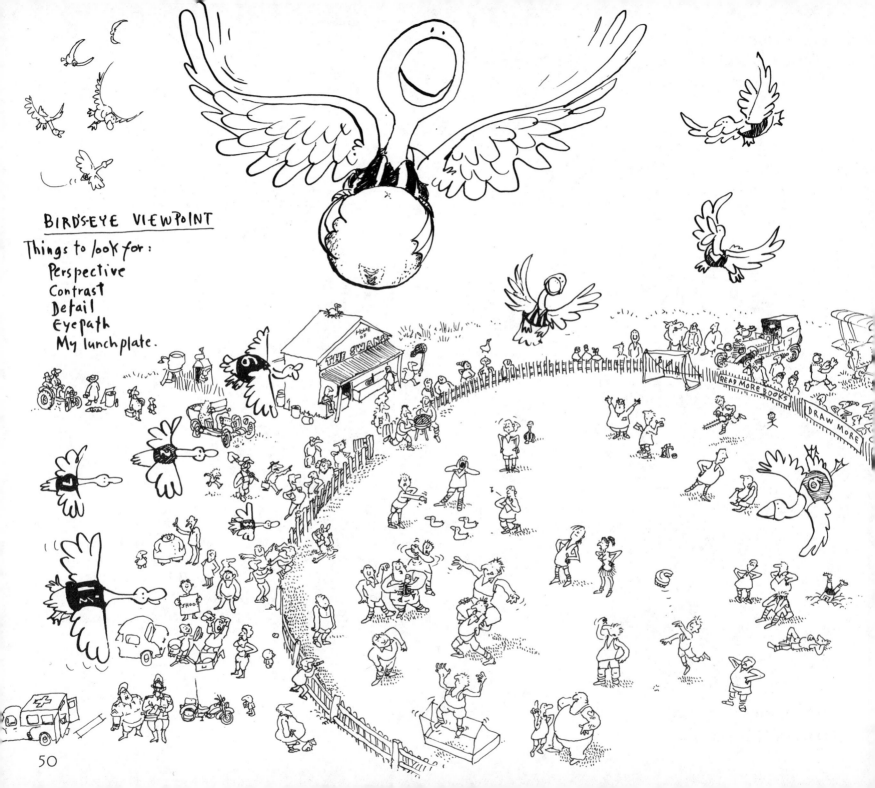

BIRD'S-EYE VIEWPOINT

Things to look for:
Perspective
Contrast
Detail
Eyepath
My lunchplate.

In worm's-eye views, the horizon, or eye-level is of course, very low.

This can be tricky to imagine, but the same rules work here too...

Lie on your back in a forest or park where there are trees. This is what a worm would see if it had glasses.

WHAT YOU SEE

Because the trees are roughly parallel to each other, they all converge to that great V.P. in the sky.

The branches and leaves are in the distance and so are very small.

UNDERGROUND NEWS

Subterranea, Mon. 'The craze of Bungy Jumping which has hit the elephant world has presented new challenges to artists,' an underground source said today. 'Only those with perspective are expected to sur-

Worm's eye VIEWS...

To do this drawing, I broke the elephant into a ball and four cylinders, with a V.P above.

I was careful at all times not to hurt it.

Sections are like a slice through something, allowing you to see what's inside it: how it works, how it's made, what's underneath the skin.

Sections are mostly used by architects and engineers to explain the structure of something for the builder. They are also used in science to show what secrets are hidden inside plants and animals, and can explain things as small as cells or as big as our planet.

I use sections to show more than I could in a normal drawing:

VIEWPOINTS
SECTION
DRAWINGS!

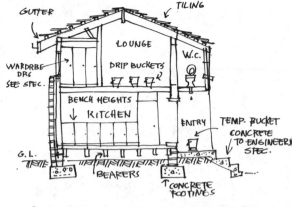

GUTTER TILING
WARDRBE DRG SEE SPEC.
LOUNGE
W.C.
DRIP BUCKETS
BENCH HEIGHTS
↓ KITCHEN
ENTRY
TEMP. BUCKET CONCRETE TO ENGINEER SPEC.
G.L.
BEARERS
CONCRETE FOOTINGS

SERIOUS SECTIONS FOR BUILDING FROM are fine for builders, but we want to do different things. So we can simplify ours like this...

I can show what goes on up here...

Must be a miner from Chiner

...and down here!

I can show the remains of ancient civilizations...

light at end of tunnel

Plastic   gold

Gold

ahh.. lunch. I thought that ice age would never end...

cubes from ice age

I think Roland Harvey drew these plans... the moat should be outside.

3-D

3-D or perspective sections are more difficult but more interesting than simple sections...

"RODNEY, GO AND SEE WHAT'S KEEPING YOUR DAD."

VP x

This section of a reversible amphibious motor home-houseboat is an example of clever design and almost impossible 3-D perspective. (available mid 1996)

© Copyright, patented and certified.

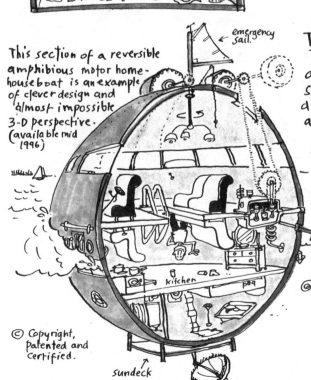

emergency sail.

sundeck

kitchen   bog

TECHNICAL SECTION DRAWINGS

It is MOST important that these drawings are completely accurate. There is no room for guesswork or sloppy drawing. Always consult your doctor before attempting this type of drawing.

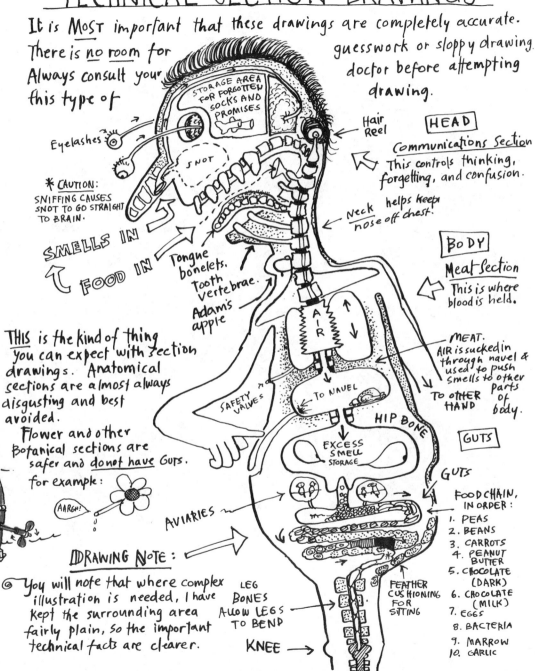

STORAGE AREA FOR FORGOTTEN SOCKS AND PROMISES

Eyelashes

SNOT

* CAUTION: SNIFFING CAUSES SNOT TO GO STRAIGHT TO BRAIN.

SMELLS IN

FOOD IN

Tongue bonelets.
Tooth vertebrae.
Adam's apple

Hair Reel

HEAD

Communications Section
This controls thinking, forgetting, and confusion.

Neck helps keep nose off chest.

BODY

Meat Section
This is where blood is held.

AIR

SAFETY VALVES

TO NAVEL

MEAT. AIR is sucked in through navel & used to push smells to other parts of body.

TO OTHER HAND

HIP BONE

EXCESS SMELL STORAGE

GUTS

GUTS

THIS is the kind of thing you can expect with section drawings. Anatomical sections are almost always disgusting and best avoided.
Flower and other botanical sections are safer and do not have guts. for example:

AARGH!

DRAWING NOTE:

You will note that where complex illustration is needed, I have kept the surrounding area fairly plain, so the important technical facts are clearer.

AVIARIES

LEG BONES ALLOW LEGS TO BEND

FEATHER CUSHIONING FOR SITTING

KNEE

FOOD CHAIN, IN ORDER:
1. PEAS
2. BEANS
3. CARROTS
4. PEANUT BUTTER
5. CHOCOLATE (DARK)
6. CHOCOLATE (MILK)
7. EGGS
8. BACTERIA
9. MARROW
10. GARLIC

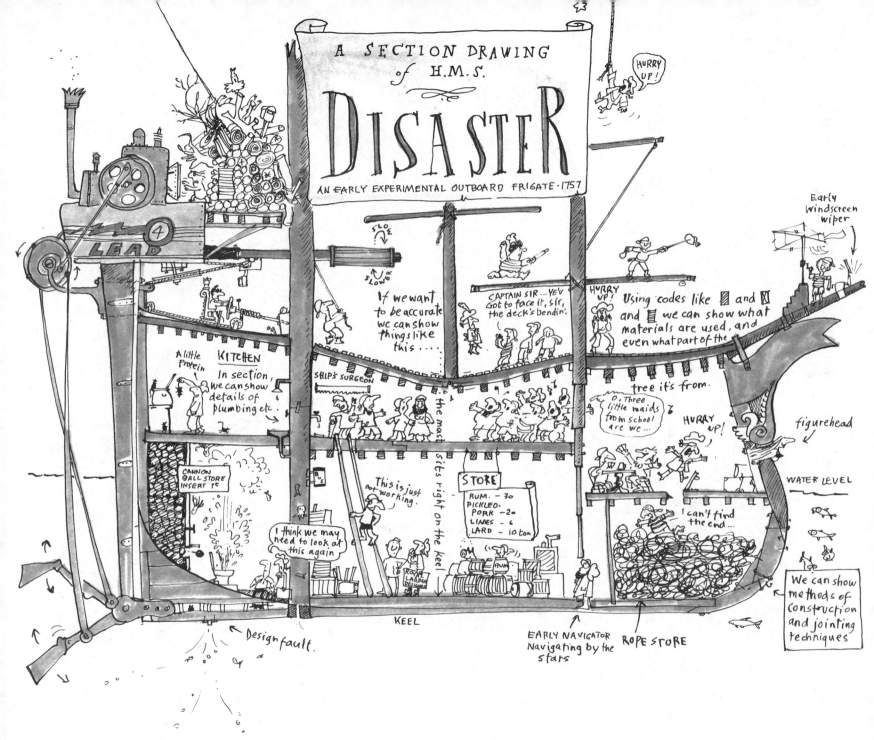

SECTION PLANNING

The first and only Golden Rule is...

You have to do things in the <u>right order</u>. Otherwise you'll end up in a bit of a mess like I did over there. So, here's where a bit of planning helps...

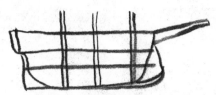

FIRST, DRAW THE SHAPE IN PENCIL... JUST BASIC STRUCTURE.

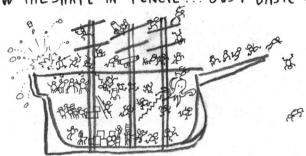

Until the figures are in place, we can't draw the background in.

SECOND, DRAW IN YOUR PEOPLE, ACTION, DETAIL. (BECAUSE NOW YOU CAN SEE

The last thing I do is to put in the tone.

WHERE TO PUT IT.) FINALLY FILL IN THE FINAL BACKGROUND AND STRUCTURE.

It was a normal day
at Lupenstein Castle ...

CROWDS

I don't know what's going on here, but you can see how much you can hide in the crowd as long as you don't break the pattern too much.

You can see the importance of contrast in getting attention in this picture.

TREES

variety is good

you can anchor them to the ground with shadows

Trees are a bit like crowds — and probably almost everything else — you don't need to draw them all perfectly!

Misty

Windy

58 Sunny

AND NOW IT'S TIME FOR... SOME TRICKS and HINTS TO HELP WITH DRAWING.

COFF COFF... PSST... WINK WINK NUDGE NUDGE

It's not always necessary to draw everything in full detail—in fact it's often best not to.

All we need is a suggestion of detail and the viewer's eye does the rest.

By using more detail, contrast or different movement to attract the viewer's eye, you can focus the viewer's attention on particular parts of your drawing.

TEXTURES

Bricks usually work like this but

REMEMBER PERSPECTIVE?

you can suggest them in other ways.

Stones are usually less organised

and grass can be either.

 orange peel

 golf peel

 rough wood

wood grain

 Neat water

 untidy water

Consider the kind of strokes to use to get the effects you want.

Being consistent is important for your drawing not to look patchy.

wrong!

ON REFLECTION...

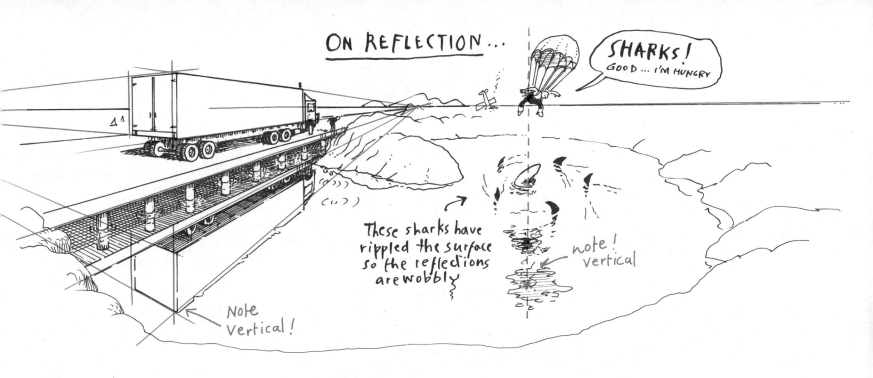

These sharks have rippled the surface so the reflections are wobbly

note! vertical

Note Vertical!

Reflections are only mirrored images in water or glass, etc (not mud).
If the surface is smooth, it's easy! Just use the same v.p. as the real thing.

RIPPLES

Ripples make reflections wobbly, which is good because you can cheat. You tend to see bits of ripple, but they're all parts of a circle.

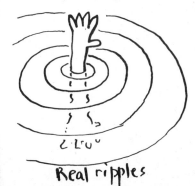

Real ripples

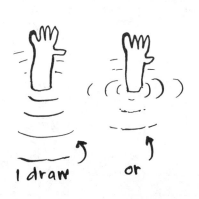

I draw   or

You can see how ellipses turn into circles as you move overhead.

Ripples tell part of the story... they show the angle you are on, in relation to the surface.

STAIRS

① Easy way.
BASIC INFORMATION:
← UP • DOWN →

They're upside-down!

STAIRS

DEGREE OF DIFFICULTY: 6.5

② Harder!
× V.P.

He's done them too big! ~

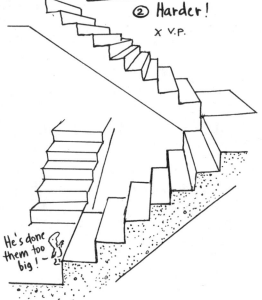

STAIRS

DEGREE OF DIFFICULTY: 10.5

③

CAUTION: SPIRAL STAIRS HAVE BEEN DECLARED DANGEROUS TO THE EYES, BRAIN AND IN EXTREME CASES CAN MAKE YOU **DIZZY!**

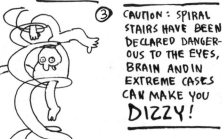

DIFF!CULT, INCREDIBLY HARD and IMPOSSIIBLE THINGS TO DRAW

I tried these spiral stairs by eye. I think if they look ok. to me, that's ok.

WHY IT'S HARD:

HERE, we're looking up at the steps.

We are looking at one spiral shape here,...

another one here

another one here

and another one here

DOWN HERE, we're looking down at the steps.

THINGS WE CAN BE FAIRLY SURE OF:

① All risers are this shape.

They are all vertical.

Their V.P. is on the same horizon.

② All treads are this shape:

Goodness knows where their V.P.'s are.

Probably left at the super-market.

③ We'll only have to draw them about once in our whole life, when we need to show off.

ON YOUR OWN

If you can do spiral stairs using VPs and rules, you should write a book.

FABRIC

SHOULD NOT BE ATTEMPTED BY PERSONS SUFFERING STRESS.

IF OVEREXPOSED STARE IMMED-IATELY AT FLAT WHITE WALL.

① Try to get the basic shape of the fabric (in pencil).

Table top.

Bottom of fabric

② Join the edges that are not hidden by the folds, to the top (in ink).

NOTE: Works on dresses also.

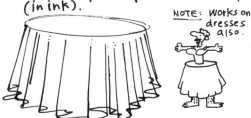

③ Ink the rest of the bottom edge except those hidden.

NOTE: And lampshades.

HELP

④ Rub out pencil when dry.

It's <u>very</u> hard to do this sort of thing with real V.Ps, but it helps to use the principle of <u>'smaller in the distance'</u>.

NEED A HAND WITH HANDS ?
Certainly sir or madam. Cheat.

At certain times in every life, there comes a test of moral strength, courage and character. The greatest of these is when we are faced with something which we just don't want to draw.

The ONLY honourable thing to do when faced with this is to CHEAT.

Dust, snow and sand can save a lot of time and labour.

BAD HAIR DAY ? TRY A HAT.

FEET A PROBLEM ? NO PROBLEM.
MUSCLES ? NOTHING TO IT !

Moo moo * moo

* Calf mussels

Mucked up the eyes in your best drawing ?

An attractive and practical answer !

Should we do the MacDonald or the Campbell tartan ?

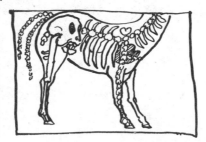

Who cares ?

There are many ways to draw horses' feet :

WRONG

WRONG

ANATOMICALLY CORRECT
USING BONES, HEART ETC.

YOU-KNOW-WHAT

He means 'summery' I think.

As you can see in this book, there are some things I draw better than others. That's fine. My drawings probably express me as an individual better than anything else! Your drawings can be the same for you. I know my best drawings are the ones I've done for me and no other purpose. If you can work out what motivates you, what blocks you up, and how you best overcome blocks, you've done well.

If a new white sheet of paper freezes you up, draw on bits of old paper. Don't worry about making mistakes, practise turning them into good things. Don't be afraid of planning: now I'm writing this conclusion THE END it's obvious that the planning had to be done before I could unblock and the jokes came along afterward as I relaxed and worked on the drawing.

So go and start working on your own style. Try as many styles, subjects and media as you can, and above all — relax and enjoy drawing.

'Bye now!

63

Now that you've enjoyed Roland Harvey's way of learning to draw, you can explore these other great books in the Young Designer Series:

The Animation Book by Peter Viska

The Calligraphy Book by Peter Grislis

The Calligraphy Book Companion by Peter Grislis

The Cartoon Book by James Kemsley

The Cartoon Book 2 by James Kemsley

The Comic Strip Book by Peter Foster

The Drawing Book by John Deacon

The Lettering Book by Noelene Morris

The Lettering Book Companion by Noelene Morris

The Photography Book by Edward Stokes

The Project Lettering Book by Robert Ainsworth.